My Child has Special Needs
A JOURNEY FROM GRIEF TO JOY

My Child has Special Needs
A JOURNEY FROM GRIEF TO JOY

Rebeckah J. Ripley

Packaged by Pleasant Word, PO Box 428, Enumclaw, WA 98022.
The views expressed or implied in this work do not necessarily
reflect those of Pleasant Word. The author is ultimately responsible
for the design, content and editorial accuracy of this work.

Verses marked NIV are taken from the Holy Bible, New International
Version, Copyright © 1973, 1978, 1984 by the International Bible
Society. Used by permission of Zondervan Publishing House. The
"NIV" and "New International Version" trademarks are registered
in the United States Patent and Trademark Office by International
Bible Society.

Verses marked NKJV are taken from the New King James
Version, © 1979, 1980, 1982 by Thomas Nelson, Inc., Publish-
ers. Used by permission.

ISBN 1-4141-0040-X
Library of Congress Catalog Card Number: 2003112743

This book is dedicated to
Gideon,
my life, my "Little Love",
my inspiration.
Being your mom is one of my life's
greatest privileges.

Contents

Acknowledgements

First, I have to say a warm, deserving, and humble thank you to my Father. Lord, you took my thoughts, my hands, and my willing heart, and you created the pages of this book. Thank you, Father, for using me.

Thank you to my husband, Adam. You were very patient with me during this journey and during the writing of this book. Your love amazes me. Thank you for the vulnerability, and thank you for allowing me to share our story.

I also wish to extend my love and thanks to Dr. and Mrs. Elroy Post, who invested a year of intense nurture and a lifetime of prayers into a child who was not their own. Thank you for teaching me what love and family is all about. Bernice, I am grateful and incredibly indebted to you for giving up your summer to grade yet another paper! Thank you for giving of yourself to edit this book. Your encouragement and skill were a generous gift to me!

And to my favorite high school teacher, Mrs. Sue Donker, *Dr. D*. With much patience and understanding, you mold young minds to appreciate the beauty of their own and others' penned words. You teach more than creative writing and literature; you teach beauty and self-worth. Thank you for breathing life into my heart and mind. Thank you for believing in me and in my writing.

I want to thank Kevin and Wendy Verstegen. Kevin, you will always be dear to my heart. You have been a source of wisdom and encouragement in my life for many years. Thank you for allowing me to use some of your words to minister hope. Wendy, you are my daisy with iron petals (Proverbs 27:17). I so greatly appreciate you and this friendship. I am so glad that He has chosen to take the broken and crumbly pieces of my life and fashion them into the most beautiful of treasures. Thank you for allowing me to use bits of your story to touch the moms who read this book.

One final thank you must be said to the individuals who gave of their time and energy to read this manuscript and give much appreciated feedback. Thank you Gwen Klein, Cindy Kirkpatrick, Katie Petros, Katie Glynn, Mark Tegtmeier, Monique Mader, Michelle Kunes, Gail Bushman, and Mary Kohler.

Introduction

If you're anything like me, though I try to find time to read, my day is filled with many other things. By the time I lie down at night, I'm too tired to pick up a book. However, I have found that there are those quiet moments in many days where I can capture time for myself, if I look for it. These moments flee quickly, but they are refreshing! The chapters in this book are intentionally short, from one mom to another. I suggest you accompany the reading of this book with a spiral to write down thoughts as they come; our minds are filled with so many other things, though we try to remember, we often forget. At the end of each chapter you will find Points to Ponder. These can be used to aid in this journey. If you are studying this book as a group, they can assist in leading the discussion. Use your spiral for the Points to Ponder as well, keeping all of your thoughts and reflections in one place. The concepts I share in this book will, hopefully, encourage you, but they are merely tools to aid in your journey.

Traveling Together,
Rebeckah

Part I

Starting Points

CHAPTER ONE

Let Me Walk a Mile With You

Do your mornings ever become a blur of rushing activity? The smoke detector lets everyone in the house know that the toast is burned again this morning. Your husband is running late for work, grumbling all the way. You're trying to coordinate your twelve-year-old's transportation to soccer practice because the family car is in the shop. You forgot to sign the permission slip, and you hope three dollars will cover lunch. "Try to get something healthy today . . ." you utter in a futile attempt to steer your child towards nutrition as he runs out the door to meet his friends heading for school.

The same chaotic whirl occurs every morning in homes across the nation, but not every home has a mom who is trying to diaper an eight-year-old while the dog barks to be let out. Not every home has a screaming five-year-old; you know he is hungry, but without any expressive language skills, you cannot figure out that he wants banana pancakes for breakfast instead of the burnt toast. Not every home has a three-year-old, fighting against taking the medicine he needs to just make it through the day. You collapse in tears. It's just too much to handle sometimes!

Do the first few hours of your day ever begin like this? I know mine have many times. I've felt so alone. I've been so overwhelmed. I've felt completely lost. So I collapse, take a few slow breaths, wipe the tears, and get up to try one more time. It's the same thing we all do.

Sometimes we get stuck in this "survival" mode, doing what we have to do so we can make it through the day. The burdens we carry are silent ones. We function, giving out so very much, that when the day is done we have nothing left for ourselves. In survival mode, the needs of our child(ren) supersede our own needs and desires. We are super-sensitive and running ragged. A flurry of days blurs itself into weeks, weeks into months, months into years. The things that used to be important to us are different now. The goals we set for our life, the "where I hope to be in five years" have been misplaced somewhere along this journey. We function to survive. We survive because that is what life demands from us. However, there is more to life than this! There is hope. There is joy. There is peace. There is rest.

Matthew 11:28–30 Come to me, all you who are weary and burdened, and I will give you rest. Take my yoke upon you and learn from me, for I am gentle and humble in heart, and you will find rest for your souls. For my yoke is easy and my burden is light.

The pages of this book started during my walk through grief. It was a way for me to process my feelings and record my journey. I have learned some amazing things along the way. Different people have come into my life to walk a mile with me as I traveled along. They have brought insight and wisdom, a road map to follow. They have brought encouragement, water to my thirsty soul. This is a journey none of us can walk alone. It is my prayer that these words give you some direction and some refreshment. It's a long journey, but you are not traveling alone.

The words and feelings in this book are very personal. It is only with the loving support of my husband, Adam, that I can even share all of this with you. As moms of special needs children, we carry a heavy load, but we are not the only ones who feel the pain. My husband has lovingly allowed me to share the very intimate and vulnerable side of parenting a child with special needs.

I have a form of ovarian disease that was diagnosed shortly before Adam and I were married. My doctor explained to us that I would have a very difficult time conceiving and carrying children to term. We fully understood this and resigned our "right" to have children, leaving it in God's hands. Our first Christmas as newly weds, we announced to our families that a miracle was going to be arriving the next summer. Several months later, Gideon was born. What a wonderful gift; life was going to be just perfect!

God bless those first-borns! I think it all starts when we pick patterns for their nursery. We have baby showers. We wash and fold their Onesies five times. We read countless books on pregnancy, childbirth, and parenting. We attend birthing classes and tour the hospital in our third trimester, even though the suitcase has been packed for three months already! We put all of our hopes and dreams and expectations into them! They will fulfill our dreams. They will accomplish what we missed out on. We want the best for them. We decide they will potty train by eighteen months and be writing poetry by age three. They will be bright students, budding musicians, and star athletes. The baby hasn't even been born yet, and here we are signing them up for piano lessons!

Now, I know we are all a little more levelheaded than that, but can't we see a tiny bit of truth in that scenario? It's humorous, but it demonstrates the expectations we have for our new little life . . . Those are all big, grandiose thoughts, so we love our children even if they don't paint quite as well as Leonardo Di Vince. There are some things, however, that are just obvious, right? All babies are supposed to be healthy. What happens when they aren't? All babies eventually learn to walk, talk, and feed themselves. What happens when they don't?

Points to Ponder:

Do you function in "survival" mode?

How long has your journey been up until now?

Who has come along side of you to give you bits of a road map?

Who has walked a mile with you, giving you water to drink?

In what ways have these individuals aided your journey?

Memorize Matthew 11:28–30

CHAPTER TWO

Right With God

Nothing in this book can be of any benefit to you without the power of God working within you. I believe life is more than just birth, all the middle stuff, and death. I believe each of us was created with a purpose. We were created for relationship with God, created for a personal, individual relationship with our loving Heavenly Father.

Before anything else can be said, the foundation of this book and the foundation of our lives need to be with Christ Jesus set in place as our cornerstone. It is true that when a house is built, a misplaced cornerstone will cause the collapse of the entire structure. A perfect cornerstone ensures a solid foundation. It is the same with our lives. I Peter, chapter 2 gives a beautiful word picture:

Verses 4–10 As you come to Him, the living Stone—rejected by men but chosen by God and precious to Him—you also, like living stones, are being built into a spiritual house to be a holy priesthood, offering spiritual sacrifices acceptable to God through Jesus Christ. For in Scripture it says: 'See, I lay a stone in Zion, a chosen and precious cornerstone, and the one who trusts in Him will never be put to shame.' [Reference to Isaiah 40:6–8] Now to you who believe, this stone is precious. But to those who do not believe, 'The stone the builders rejected has become the capstone' (or cornerstone). [Reference to Psalm 118:22] and 'A stone that causes men to stumble and a rock that makes them fall.' [Reference to Isaiah 8:14] They stumble because they disobey the message—which is also what they were destined for.

But you are a chosen people, a royal priesthood, a holy nation, a people belonging to God, that you may declare the praises of Him who called you out of darkness into His wonderful light. Once you were not a people, but now you are the people of God; once you had not received mercy, but now you have received mercy.

Verses 15–16 For it is God's will that by doing good you should silence the ignorant talk of foolish men. Live as free men, but do not use your freedom as a cover-up for evil; live as servants of God.

Long before this world began to spin on its perfectly crafted axis, there was God. John 1:1–5 says, *In the beginning was the Word, and the Word was with God, and the Word was God. He was with God in the beginning. Through Him all things were made; without Him nothing was made that has been made. In Him was life, and that life was the light of men. The light shines in the darkness, but the darkness has not understood it.*

God created us, gave us a beautiful, flawless, environment that cared for all of our needs. There was no hunger, no pain, no fear, no sickness, and no death. God did not want us to be robots, controlled by the flick of His finger, so He also gave us a free will. What a beautiful gift the Creator fashioned us with! With that free will, we were given the option whether or not we wanted to love God, our Father and Maker.

Adam and Eve exercised their right to choose. They chose to disobey God. With that, they began to understand the difference between life and death. For centuries men continued to exercise their right to choose, and men continued to suffer the consequences of that choice. *For all have sinned and fallen short of the glory of God.* (Romans 3:23)

So our loving Father, our maker, sent His son, Jesus, into the world. John 1 continues in verse 14, *The Word became flesh and made His dwelling among us. We have seen His glory, the glory of the One and Only, who came from the Father, full of grace and truth.*

Jesus came to pay the penalty of our sin. He was blameless. He did nothing wrong. He did not deserve death. However, His amazing love for you and for me drove Him to give His own life in place of ours. He paid the debt of the sin we owed. Romans 6:23 explains, *For the wages of sin is death, but the gift of God is eternal life in Christ Jesus our Lord.*

We were created for relationship with God. He loves you! Romans 5:8 puts it this way: *God demonstrated His own love for us in this: While we were still sinners, Christ died for us.*

WOW! What an amazing love He has for us! Whether we choose to accept this gift or not, He surrendered His life for me and for you, so that when we do die, we do not have to spend an eternity in Hell. I once heard Hell defined as "Separation from God." We were created for relationship with Him; when we are not fulfilling our purpose in life, we are miserable. Our created purpose is relationship with Christ. God gave us a free will; it is our free will to choose to follow our created purpose or continue running from our Creator.

If you haven't made the choice to accept Christ to be your personal Lord and Savior, would you consider making that choice today? When you are ready, speak your heart to your Father who loves you so much. Following is a prayer you can use, if you would like to. Why don't you first read through it and ponder the meaning of the words? Then speak the words aloud as a prayer; He is listening.

Dear Father in Heaven,

I know that You created me with a purpose. I know Your purpose for my life is to have a relationship with You. I have sinned. I have fallen short. My life has not honored You. The penalty of my sin is death. Without your forgiveness, I know that I will spend an eternity in separation from You. I am sorry for the things I have done and for the ways in which I have hurt you. I need your forgiveness. I know that Jesus Christ died on the cross to pay the penalty for my sins. Would you please pardon my sins and remember them no more? I want to fulfill my purpose in life. I want to have

*a relationship with You. I put my life into Your hands. Thank
you for Your love. Thank you for Your forgiveness.*

In Your Holy name I pray, Jesus.

Amen

Luke 15:10 says, *There is rejoicing in the presence of the
angels of God over one sinner who repents.* Heaven is rejoicing over you right now!

Now that you have made a decision to live your life,
fulfilling your purpose and destiny, there are a couple of
things you must do. Think of it this way: A plant that is not
watered will die. A baby that is not fed will die. A new
Christian who is not discipled will not grow or develop
spiritually.

First, you must tell someone. Whether you tell the girl
at work that has been praying for you for months, or you
call a pastor from your town, you need to tell someone!

Secondly, you must get a Bible and read it. Read your
Bible every day. Read it with hunger to learn more about
your Creator and more about your purpose in this life. There
are many very good translations published. The New King
James Version, the Revised Standard Version, and the New
International Version are all very understandable. The Living Bible, or other paraphrased versions of Scripture, break
it down and make the reading simpler to understand. Whatever version you choose, get it and get reading! A good
place to start is the book of John in the New Testament.

The next step is finding a church where you can meet
with other Christians. I hope that there is a quality, bal-

anced, Bible-believing, Bible-teaching church near you. Get involved. Join a Bible study. Talk to the pastor about discipleship classes. Continue to pursue God.

Welcome to the family.

Points to Ponder:

Describe your relationship with God.

Be honest and describe how you feel when you think about God, your Creator.

Do you believe that God created your child? How does that thought make you feel?

Read and memorize Psalm 139:13–16

Part II

Permission to Grieve

CHAPTER THREE

Grieving the Birth

Picture it with me: A new mother lies in her warm hospital bed as the nurse gently hands her this tiny, tightly bundled, little angel. "Absolutely perfect!" the mother whispers as she gazes into the captivating eyes of her newly born child.

I don't know about you, but my birth experience was much different. I wasn't even in labor when the OB was called to the hospital to perform emergency surgery to save the life of my baby.

I was wheeled into the operating room. I was anxious and trying to do my best to keep in good spirits, but I was getting a bit frustrated with the anesthesiologist who was rather impatient that day. "Maybe he's late for a dinner party," I thought, trying to give him the benefit of the doubt. "But excuse me, I'm just trying to have a baby here!"

Quickly my husband entered the room and took my hand. Was this it? Is this how nine months of planning is about to end? What about the birth classes we took? At least I don't have to try to remember to breathe.

What was happening?

Is the baby okay?

I lost consciousness; I think that was a good thing.

I awoke in the recovery room. "Where is my husband?" I asked the nurse. "He's with the baby." I wanted to see my baby, but I couldn't. The nurses were working with him.

I was brought to my room and transferred into bed. By that time Adam's parents had arrived at the hospital, eager new grandparents. Amid the flurry of activity, I remember wanting to see our son, but I kept being told the nurses were with him.

I felt frustrated because I did not understand what was happening. I was still feeling the effects of the drugs, and I don't remember a whole lot of what happened. Adam tried to protect me as much as he could by not sharing a lot of the detail of that first evening until I was out of the hospital. To this day, when Adam speaks of the first hours of Gideon's life, his eyes well up with tears. The feelings of fear and anxiety, and the brutal awareness that his baby son might have died that night, evoke deep pain for him; this memory is an immense ache in his heart.

I will never forget the first time I was able to hold him that night. His perfect little body mesmerized me. "They're all here . . ." I sighed in relief as I counted his teeny fingers and itty-bitty toes. He was *perfect*. Everything was normal. The crisis was behind us; it was all going to be okay.

The following day I began to understand that everything was not going to be normal . . .

Gideon had gone into fetal distress; the pediatrician told us we would not know the long-term effects of the oxygen deprivation for three to five years.

At birth, Gideon's blood glucose measured only ten but should have been sixty or higher. With his glucose in the critical range, we did around the clock feeding every hour and a half. I was very determined to nurse. To the horror of Adam and me, the nursing staff wanted to put in a feeding tube. We begged them not to. One nurse took our side; it was no accident that she was on the floor that night. She sat down and patiently taught us how to feed Gideon with a syringe. We would alternate formula and nursing. This seemed to be working. His blood sugar was slowly rising. They tested his glucose level several times each day; his feet were completely black and blue from the needle pricks. I finally asked them to take him out of the room when they did the test because I wept to see him in so much pain.

Things seemed to be looking up . . . that was until the pediatrician came to tell us he would have to stay a little longer. His billirubbin was rising quickly, causing him to become jaundiced. This was nothing to worry about, she assured us.

Finally, Gideon was released from the hospital with a billi-blanket to be worn around the tummy at home. We felt completely blessed to have him out so quickly, considering all that he had been through. It was a Sunday afternoon, Adam's first day back to work, when I made an urgent call to the pediatrician; Gideon's urine was such a deep orange, it looked almost red in the diaper. My mother-in-law brought us to the hospital; Adam would meet us in the Emergency Department.

Looking at the lab report, the ER doctor told us Gideon needed to be admitted. Though his glucose was still low, it was stable. The billirubbin, however, had risen significantly. They wheeled us (I had just had major abdominal surgery) to the special care nursery where they put Gideon in an isolette. We could only touch him every three hours when I nursed.

I felt so broken. There was my tiny baby boy locked in that terrible box. For nine months I had longed to hold him, kiss him, rock him, and sing to him as he slept in my arms. Now all I could do was look at him from outside of a plastic box. I began to hate that box! It was cold and indifferent. It did not realize that it was holding my baby. It felt the touch and warmth that I longed to feel. It was keeping me from holding my child, but at the same time I realized that this box was doing all it could to help my baby; it was helping my son fight for his life.

The nursing staff gave me a small room to "nest" and rest during Gideon's stay. It was during that time of rest when the hospital's program came on television about grieving the birth experience. It gave me the permission I needed to mourn what was supposed to be a "blessed event."

To grieve the birth experience meant to face the reality of it. Adam and I had talked about a natural birth (we were naive first-timers!). We had discussed who was going to be present during the birth. We had taken the classes and toured the hospital. What happened?

I felt like I wasn't a real mom. Real moms have seemingly endless hours of labor pains. Real moms scream and cry when the pain becomes too intense. Real moms push.

Real moms feel the child as it leaves her body. I experienced none of that.

I've always felt that anything worth having in life is worth working for. Adam and I did not work to get pregnant; we did not use fertility drugs, monitor my temperature, or exhaust our resources in an attempt to conceive. This pregnancy was a gift to us! Frankly, I struggled with my emotions during the pregnancy. The timing was not my own. I was scared and unsure. I felt guilty for feeling this way, but I knew that I would love my child no matter how afraid of failure I was. I knew one thing I would have to go through was the birth, and I knew that would be hard. I knew that would be work. I thought I might somehow redeem my ambivalence during pregnancy with a long, difficult delivery. I felt like I needed to pay for my uncertainty and prove that I wanted this child and that I could be a good mom. Now I had the baby, but I hadn't worked for that either. How could I be this child's mother? It was nothing that I had worked for. He was just handed to me.

I felt as if I had not given birth; my obstetrician birthed my child. I wasn't there for him when they gave him injections of glucose to increase his blood sugar or poked him for tests to monitor his glucose levels. My journey of motherhood to this point had been so short, and already I felt like a complete failure. To add to my guilt, I was told that one possible reason for the rise in billirubin was that he might not be nursing correctly. "Oh, great!" I thought, "The one thing I *can* do for him—I can't do right!"

I really needed to grieve. This birth had not been as I expected; it was quite traumatic for me and for Gideon. I was angry that life couldn't be normal. I was angry with myself. "It has to be my fault somehow," I thought. I was faced with the reality that I could not be the perfect mom I had hoped to be. I was disappointed in the experience and disappointed in myself. I felt like a failure. Motherhood was not supposed to be like this. This was all wrong! Or was it?

> *Jeremiah 29:11 says "For I know the plans I have for you,"*
> *declares the Lord. "Plans to prosper you, not to harm you.*
> *Plans to give you hope and a future."*

How in the midst of the pain can I cling to a promise that God's plans are not intended to harm me? How can all of this drama fit into God's plans for Gideon, to prosper him and not harm him? That is part of the journey I want to walk with you.

Points to ponder:

What were your expectations of your child's birth?

Take a few moments to briefly write out the events of your child's birth.

Was it a typical delivery?

Was it traumatic?

Describe the moment you first held your newborn child.

Do you need to mourn the birth?

Memorize Jeremiah 29:11

CHAPTER FOUR

Grieving the Diagnosis

As moms, we all have our own, very unique story of the birth of our child. However, we all relate to other birth stories in the common threads that weave between them. As moms of children with special needs, we have individual diagnoses, prognoses, and quality of life. However, our heartache, anger, and answerless inquiries are common, and I want you to know that they are okay!

Maybe your first gaze at your child revealed a physical defect.

Perhaps your doctor's words were prefaced with a compassionate, "I'm sorry . . ."

Maybe your child's birth was very typical, but an accident caused damage physically or mentally.

Whatever the cause, here we are. We are not just mothers. We are nurses. Whatever our child's physical disability may be, we are specialists in that field. Not by choice. Personally, I know more about the digestive system and diseases of the bowel than I ever wanted to know. We are pharmacists. Do you laugh when asked, "What has your child taken for this?" I usually offer the What-he-hasn't-taken list. That one is much shorter. We are Central Scheduling. With doctor appointments, visits to the specialist, and therapy added to the schedule of everyone else in the family, the calendar is a flood of ink scribble. For those of us who have a child with developmental delays, we get crash courses in physical, occupational, and/or speech therapy. We quickly proceed from the under-graduate degree in parenting and are thrust immediately into the doctorate program.

Motherhood is hard! Raising children with good health and typical development is difficult. Have you ever walked through the parenting aisle of your local Christian bookstore? There are endless resources for raising children: how to encourage them, how to teach them God's word, how to discipline them, how to love them. Motherhood is even more difficult when your child has special needs.

As we discussed in Chapter One, we have expectations for our child. We recognize that most of these expectations are not conscious thoughts until we view them and give them a name. We want the very best for our children, so of course we expect them to be healthy. Obviously we anticipate normal growth and development. We look forward to being a part of their lives as they reach each milestone. We look forward to kissing them goodbye on their first day of school. We dream of their high school graduation and sending them off to college. We think about what their spouse will be like. We love to dream about their wedding day and the births of their children. These are all real thoughts, dreams, and anticipations we have for our children. They are normal. We dream the very best for our children because we want the very best for them. We love our kids. There is nothing wrong with that! A friend once told me, "It's okay to build castles in the sky as long as you don't live in them."

However, there comes a point when those expectations are shattered. For some, that comes as early as prenatal screening, when the obstetrician delivers the results of the test. For others, it comes at birth. For some, it may come in the form of a conference with your child's teacher when she suggests you go for specialized testing.

What has happened? Our hopes and dreams are beginning to crack and crumble. Life, as we anticipated it to be, is no longer reality. There has been a change in our lives. We did not want this change. We do not like this change, but we know there is no going back to the way things used to be. What do we do with all the pain we feel?

Like grieving the birth, we need to grieve the diagnosis. The first step in grieving started for me one day while in heartbreak and frustration, I confided to my father-in-law, "I feel as though I need to grieve the loss of the expectations I have of a child with normal health and development." I felt so much freedom in simply putting that hurt into words. I had been feeling it for quite some time, but I was having trouble expressing it. I was also feeling some guilt for viewing the precious life of my child through the eyes of sorrow.

Confessing my vulnerability, I once wrote, "Life seems to be moving from one period of grieving to the next period of grieving, and I think I should stay in this particular grief a little longer since I don't want to know what my next loss is going to be." I, personally, have had a lot of loss in my life. My mother died of breast cancer when I was ten years old. My grandpa died of lung cancer when I was thirteen, and my grandma died of congestive heart failure when I was twenty-three years old. Grief is something I have known very well. I continued my vulnerability by penning these words, "My current grief involves the death of my expectations of a 'normal' child. This summer our son took on a new label: "developmentally disabled." This happened the year Gideon turned three, and what a long three years they had been!

At three weeks of age Gideon was diagnosed with Reflux Disease, the beginning of his gastrointestinal problems. The diagnosis process was an incredibly long one; by the time he reached his third birthday, he had been through countless tests and procedures, two requiring general anesthesia.

Gideon was put on a very rigid vegan diet, until he received his final diagnosis. What a shock this was to me, a girl who was raised on frozen pizza and fast food. Shopping was completely different; I had to painfully venture into this thing called the "Produce Section." It was not an easy adjustment for any of us, but we struggled through, and we all made it out alive (and a little healthier!). Just before his fourth birthday, we received a much needed answer. Gideon was diagnosed with Celiac Disease, an autoimmune disease of the small intestines which causes foods to go through undigested, unabsorbed, and with great pain. When Celiac children have developmental delays, it compounds the problem of proper diagnosis.

At his two year physical I asked the pediatrician if she thought his speech was appropriate for his age. She thought he may be a little delayed and referred us to our county Birth To Three program (every county in the U.S. is required to have this program). Gideon received speech therapy and, later, early-childhood services through this program.

The summer he turned three, he was referred to the school district, who did more extensive testing and determined that his cognitive developmental delays were significant enough to qualify for Early Childhood Education, preschool for children with special needs. Before the Celiac diagnosis, we suspected Gideon had a mild form of autism. So much of our struggle stemmed from the behavioral, developmental, and temperamental issues we were trying so desperately to understand. We are curious to see how this temperament plays out in adulthood.

Gideon's Early Childhood teacher told me, "There are easy children, and there are difficult children." With a grin she finished, "... *and Gideon is not easy!*" He is a very determined child; he has always been that way. He has a lot of strength in his temperament. As a first-time mom, I was hoping for a compliant child, but God knew our family better than that! Gideon's feistiness and intensity are gifts to him and to us. During the struggles, it was often difficult to keep this in perspective, but I don't think that he would be where he is today if it were not for his tenacity.

For me, the grieving process began with admitting to myself and then speaking it out loud, that my son, though a wonderful gift from God, was not a "typical" child. Gideon is special. He is on a special diet. He has a serious medical condition. He received a lot of therapy and attended special education classes. Though, at the same time, Gideon is very functional. I felt guilty for thinking of him as "special needs" because he does not have Downs Syndrome or Autism. He is not in a wheel chair; he is not crippled. He will grow up and, hopefully, have a happy, successful adult life. However, to rob myself of the permission to say Gideon does have special needs only hurts our family. It robs me of validation of all that I am feeling. It robs Adam and Gideon of that same thing, too. It could also have kept Gideon from receiving the help that he needed.

As we walked through the understanding of Gideon's delays, there were more things that we needed to grieve. Sometimes it felt as if we were taking a step or two back so that we could try to move ahead in a better direction for Gideon. Proverbs 22:6 encourages parents to train up a child in the way he should go, or as I've heard commentated, "according to his bent." For our family, it meant taking some practical steps to help facilitate Gideon's developmental growth, regardless of how un-age-appropriate that was to do. One example I can share has to do with a teething toy.

We all know that infants put things in their mouths as part of their exploration of the world. Babies like to chew on teething rings (and anything else they manage to fit into their mouths); it has a soothing effect. This is okay for a nine-month-old. However, our son, at three years, was still putting everything in his mouth, including hands, clothes, toys, books, puzzle pieces, blocks, sticks, sand, flowers . . . I thought this behavior might be a little odd, but what did I know? I didn't have any other children, but the other three-year-olds I observed never did things like that.

At Gideon's first parent-teacher conference, his teacher and speech pathologist brought up the issue of oral sensitivity. They suggested we give him one certain object that he can use to gain the oral stimulation he needed. At school, his teacher wanted to tie a plastic tubing around his chest with a large tied knot that he could bite, chew, and suck on. My husband and I found the idea a bit barbaric, and my husband made it clear that he did not want that tied onto Gideon every day in school. The speech pathologist suggested a massaging teething toy.

Adam was against the idea because he was uncomfortable with stepping back to an earlier developmental stage. Together we discussed our thoughts and feelings on the issue. Adam felt Gideon was fine the way things were. We were both a little embarrassed and frustrated to be giving a baby toy to our pre-school child. I immediately searched for ways to blame myself, but I knew that I had done the best I could; this delay was not my fault. We finally agreed to just go to the store and see what they had to offer.

As we looked through the teething and vibrating toys, we found the specific massaging teether the speech pathologist was referring to us. We agreed to give it a try. We did not show Gideon how to use it, but he immediately picked up the toy, put it in his mouth, and to his delight, when he bit down, the toy began to vibrate. This is a toy we only used at home. We used it as a tool to show Gideon that some things were appropriate to be put in the mouth and some things were not. This gave him the oral stimulation that he needed and had a very soothing effect on him. In time we were able to phase the teething toy out. However, we were grateful that we decided to take a couple steps back so that we could move ahead in a direction that was best for Gideon, according to his bent.

Points to Ponder:

What did you anticipate for the life of your child? Give
each of those unconscious expectations a name.

How long was the diagnosis process for your child?

How do you think the idea of raising your child "according to his bent" would make a difference in your
family?

Do you feel like you have ever had to take a step or two
back so that you could move ahead in a direction
that would be better for your child?

Memorize Proverbs 22:6

CHAPTER FIVE

Silencing the Critics

I don't know which was worse: the mindless stares at Gideon's behavior, the hands that would fly up to cover ears when he let out one of his ear-piercing screams, or the comments people would make.

As a young child, Gideon had a difficult time adjusting to new situations. He demanded structure, routine, and repetition; he had a difficult time processing new sounds, objects, activities, etc. For example, we would have to go in the same door at the grocery store; otherwise, he would get very upset because he did not understand where we were going or what was happening to him.

Gideon was turning three when he took his first air plane ride to Grandma and Grandpa's house. Gideon slept, ate, or screamed. He did not understand what we were doing; this was very new and different. He did not understand why he had to stay in his seat, and screamed, "Lemmee owww! (Let me out!)" There was no reasoning with him. Needless to say, when he was awake, we tried to keep his mouth full! There was another boy, Gideon's age, on the flight in the seat behind us, and an elderly couple sat in the seats ahead of us. As we were leaving the plane, the older woman looked at the little boy who sat quietly and praised him for being such a good boy. Then she looked at Gideon and shamed him for being a "bad boy!" She was a passing stranger, and I chose to restrain myself, but I turned to Gideon and said, "Even though your behavior was not appropriate for the plane ride, I want you to know that Daddy and I love you. You are not a bad boy. Your behavior was wrong, but that does not make you a bad boy."

There are times we need to step in and silence the critics. I do not mean to say we should get in their faces, but I do mean to not let it in. For all the thoughtless stares and unkind words, I give this advice: stop them before they sink into your heart. It's not about you; it's not about your child. It is solely about the other person's own issues and insecurities. People stare because it is something they are not used to seeing. People comment out of their ignorance. You know your child like no one else on this planet. You are an expert in the moods, movements, and meaning of everything your child does. Don't let some insensitive comment make you question your competency. You are responsible for your own words and actions; you are not responsible for someone else's reaction.

Comments from ignorant people can wound us, but sometimes the hurt is from well meaning comments. When we are walking through grief, or functioning in survival, we tend to be more sensitive to the things people say. It's as if we dismiss the encouragement and assume a personal attack.

"He looks so healthy!"

"He seems fine to me."

"Don't worry. Boys are slower than girls; he'll catch up."

I have heard those words many times, and I was wounded every time. I felt as if those comments were robbing me of the validity of my feelings. I felt as if they were trying to tell me that they didn't believe he was really sick. I felt as if they were attacking me for sending him to Early Childhood Education. I felt shamed for being concerned about his health and development.

In corresponding with a friend one time, I had mentioned that Gideon was receiving therapy because of some developmental delays. This friend had not seen Gideon since he was thirteen months old. At the time of this letter, he was three. My friend responded with compassion and empathy. She was sorry to hear the news, and added, "He certainly seemed fine when we saw him."

I was hurt, and I vented to my husband, "She has not seen him in two years! I'm glad the fact that he sat in a high chair through dinner, ate some cereal and a few french fries, chewed on a toy and tried to grab everything in sight led her to the conclusion that Gideon's development is perfectly normal and he does not need help now!" I continued in sarcasm, "She's right! Let's take him out of school! Stop the speech therapy! He's fine!" My gentle husband assured me her intent was not to hurt me and brought me back down into reality.

Looking back at my over-reaction, I see that I clearly missed all the words of care, kindness, and understanding. I immediately took my defense stance and turned her words from a verbal hug into a piercing arrow. Until I was made conscious-aware of how I was hurting myself, I would receive all comments and filter them through my defensiveness and pain.

By God's design, I am a deep feeler. I am a sensitive, compassionate person. In the depths of my own grief, I did not share a lot of the daily hurt with friends because I found that people just didn't seem to get it. People usually don't understand because they only see glimpses. They don't walk through the daily struggle. They do not have any concept of the pain, frustration, and discouragement. Some people truly do speak out of their ignorance.

A dear friend was talking with me late one evening, and we were discussing this very thing. She asked why I didn't share the pain much. I explained that people just reach a limit; they get to a point where they don't want to hear it any more, it seemed to me. They come to a place where they've heard enough. It becomes almost old, a broken record, questions without many answers. They don't know what to say. They don't know how to encourage. Out of their own sadness, frustration, or guilt they give comments that cut your heart or ask questions that leave you even more confused.

Despite the fact that I had just finished explaining this to my friend, she began to get rather worked up as I proceeded to share about Gideon's delays. This woman, in her late 40's, does not have children. She was never intimately involved in the cognitive development of a small child.

First she blamed the teacher for these delays, stating that the teacher who evaluated Gideon must not have known what she was talking about (despite the fact that the teacher had been doing early childhood testing on two and three year olds for twenty years). She blamed the school district, stating their criteria are too rigid for children of such a young age. She blamed society, saying that we expect children to grow up too quickly and demand that they know more than their brains can handle. She concluded that Gideon is a genius, simply processing his world on a different plane than other children his age. Instead of services to hopefully enable him to catch up to his peers, I should simply allow him to grow at his own pace. I felt in essence that she was then blaming me; I was not allowing his development to progress naturally, rather putting him in an unyielding box to which he must conform.

Needless to say, I was devastated! I could not believe what I was hearing. She carried on with this for some time, but finally stopped to ask me what I thought.

My face must have appeared horrified; my heart was crushed! I told her how damaging her words were. We talked for quite a while about this. After understanding to what extent she had hurt me, she asked for forgiveness and said she hoped this would not mean that I would refrain from sharing with her about our struggles with Gideon. I told her that I did, indeed, forgive her, but it would take time to rebuild that trust. I perceived her comments as terribly thoughtless and insensitive.

I did not need a fix to the problems we were having; I just needed someone to listen to me. I continued to share some of my struggles with this friend because I needed someone to walk with me; carrying the burden silently was tearing me up inside. As I continued in vulnerability, my friend continued to wound me, much to my dismay. She did not understand Gideon's delays and refused to soften her heart and show compassion. Eventually, with great sorrow, I did have to separate myself from her in the midst of the pain because she was not someone that I could feel safe with. This was an astoundingly painful time. I felt so alone.

I learned two very valuable lessons through that time: First, I cannot be an emotional black hole, sucking every hurt into the abyss of pain. I need to determine if the pain is the result of my sensitivity or the product of the other person's insensitivity. Then I need to deal with the pain, either with reason and reality or by lovingly discussing it with the one who wounded me (since the wound was most likely unintentional).

Secondly, I need to keep in mind what is best for Gideon, and that is being realistic about his needs and getting the best help that we can. I need to realize that Gideon is not bad or broken; he is just different, and God chose me to be his mom. I need to do everything in my power to facilitate his growth and development. Through this trying time, I need to surround myself with positive influences and people who are going to pull me up and not pull me down. This woman was a dear friend; this loss was immensely painful.

Is it not just like our Father to bring what we need in the exact moment that we need it most? God did provide for me. He led me to share this pain with a very dear friend named Wendy. Wendy is married but has no children. I feared she would be as understanding and as compassionate as my other friend was. However, Wendy has a unique perspective because she grew up in a home with a quadriplegic father and paraplegic brother. She, with a degree in psychology, and her husband, Kevin, a pastor, were very key in my grief process. I share more about Kevin and Wendy in future chapters.

The pain and heartache are so very real and leave us feeling desperate at times. What do we do with the daily frustrations? What do we do when we are hurt and don't know where to turn? I have found there are three safe places for me to go.

One place is my husband. I find that when I go to him and lovingly initiate dialogue about my day, not only am I able to release some of my feelings, but it gives him an opportunity to share how he is feeling too. Now, the how-to of lovingly initiating a conversation with your husband is a whole other book in itself, but I will give a brief thought. Lay down your right to say anything and everything that is heavy on your heart and swirling through your mind. Go with the intent to build a bridge from your heart to your husband's heart, crossing over the muck that you've been walking through all day long. This requires much more listening than talking, and that can be hard for us moms sometimes. I had a psychology professor who used to say, "God gave you two ears and one mouth; use them proportionately!"

The second place I go to is a journal. I keep a journal on the computer where I go to process my thoughts in long narrative form. I also keep a small journal beside my bed. When I lie in bed at night, and the events of the day keep me awake, or the ideas of things I need to do tomorrow are busy in my brain, I take out that little book and jot down thoughts, often chaotic and in random form. For some reason, putting those down on paper makes it easier for me to sleep.

The third place I go (which is truly my first place to go) is my loving, understanding, all-knowing Heavenly Father. Sometimes I need a safe place to "let it all out." He understands me because He created me. He hears what I'm saying even when the words get all messed up. He listens to my heart. He cries with me. He rejoices with me. He understands my anger. He knows my frustrations. He is the resting-place I can go to; He is the place I can be completely vulnerable. He created me to need Him; what a wonderful thought that is! One of my favorite comfort verses is found in Zephaniah 3:17. *The Lord your God is with you, he is mighty to save. He will take great delight in you, he will quiet you with his love, he will rejoice over you with singing.*

Points to Ponder:

Have you ever been hurt by a well-intended comment?
Have you been the receiver of insensitive comments?
How did you respond?
Have you made the decision to forgive the person who
   hurt you?
Where are your "safe places" to be vulnerable?
Memorize Zephaniah 3:17

CHAPTER SIX

Hurts Too Much to Hope

Gideon suffered in pain for nearly four years before his diagnosis; the doctors tried to help him, but they had exhausted their means of treatment and diagnostic tests. When he was two and a half, with no diagnosis in sight, I wrote the following poem which I bitterly entitled:

The Doctor Says We Are Doing All That Can Be Done . . .

I wake to the cries of my little boy;
That sound is all too common in this place.
I wait just a moment before rising
But find him with tears flowing down his face.
I embrace his small frame, though limp and weak.
I cuddle him, kissing his precious head.
His eyes meet mine, the pain is evident.
He speaks clearly, though not one word is said.
His body jerks away, he curls up tight.

He closes his eyes and tries to be strong.
He's learned to live with pain. He falls asleep
As I rub his back and sing him this song:
"When Jesus is my portion, a constant friend is He
His eye is on the sparrow, and I know He watches me."
I offer no comfort but my presence;
I feel so helpless battling the pain.
I crawl back in bed as tears flood my eyes,
Knowing tomorrow we'll do it all again.

When the discouragement, frustration, and anguish seems to be more than we can handle, what do we do? When we find ourselves with nowhere to go, no one to listen, no one who understands, where do we turn?

Remember our scripture from Matthew 11? Jesus is speaking and says, *Come to me all you who are weary and burdened, and I will give you rest.*

When discouragement comes, we need to run, full speed, into the love of Christ. Pray! Talk to your Heavenly Father about the pain. Read! Fill your heart and mind with the truths from God's Word.

Sometimes the title waves of life rush over our hearts and minds and leave us drowning, but God has not abandoned us. He has not left us without hope.

Psalm 42 As the deer pants for streams of water, so my soul pants for you, O God. My soul thirsts for God, for the living God. When can I go and meet with God? My tears have been my food day and night while men say to me all day long, "Where is your God?" These things I remember as I pour out my soul; how I used to go with the multitude, lead-

ing the procession to the house of God, with shouts of joy and thanksgiving among the festive throng.

Why are you downcast, O my soul? Why so disturbed within me? Put your hope in God, for I will yet praise him, my Savior and my God. My soul is downcast within me; therefore I will remember you from the land of the Jordan, the heights of Hermon—from Mount Mizar. Deep calls to deep in the roar of your waterfalls; all your waves and breakers have swept over me. By day the Lord directs his love, at night his song is with me—a prayer to the God of my life.

I say to God my Rock, "Why have you forgotten me? Why must I go about mourning, oppressed by the enemy?" My bones suffer mortal agony as my foes taunt me, saying to me all day long, "Where is your God?"

Why are you downcast, O my soul? Why so disturbed within me? Put your hope in God, for I will yet praise him, my Savior and my God.

When we find ourselves in the mire of misery, nothing can pull us out besides the hope we have in Christ. Hope gives wings to our faith. Lamentations 3:21–25 says it beautifully:

Yet this I call to mind and therefore I have hope: Because of the Lord's great love we are not consumed, for his compassions never fail. They are new every morning; great is your faithfulness. I say to myself, "The Lord is my portion; therefore I will wait for him." The Lord is good to those whose hope is in him, to the one who seeks him.

It was in frustration and pain that I searched the scriptures for hope. I was so broken that I didn't even have words to pray. One evening I sat down and found six scriptures that I copied into my prayer journal and entitled each one "A Prayer for Gideon." As I daily prayed these over my son, I noticed an immediate change in me, and I know that a life long impact was made (and is being made) in Gideon's life. I want to share the prayers with you. You can substitute your child's name for Gideon's.

A Prayer for Gideon
Taken from Ephesians 1:16–19

Father,

I will not stop giving thanks for Gideon and remembering him in my prayers. I keep asking that the God of our Lord Jesus Christ, the glorious Father, may give Gideon the spirit of wisdom and revelation, so that he may know You better. I pray also that the eyes of his heart may be enlightened in order that Gideon may know the hope to which You have called him, the riches of Your glorious inheritance in the saints, and Your incomparably great power for those of us who believe.

Thank you, Father!

In Christ's name I pray,

Amen

A Prayer for Gideon
Taken from John 17:6–17

Father,

Gideon is Yours; You gave him to Adam and to me. We know that everything we have has been given to us by You. I pray for Gideon. I do not pray for the world but for the one You have given me, for he is Yours. All I have is Yours. And all You have is mine. Holy Father, protect him by the power of Your name—the name of Jesus Christ—so that our family may be one. I pray that Gideon may have the full measure of Your joy within him. I pray that You protect Gideon from the evil one. Sanctify Gideon by the truth; Your word is truth. In Your name I pray these things,

Amen.

A Prayer for Gideon
Taken from Philippians 1:9–11

Father,

This is my prayer: that Gideon's love may abound more and more in knowledge and depth of insight, so that Gideon may be able to discern what is best and may be pure and blameless until the day of Christ, filled with the fruit of righteousness that comes through Jesus Christ—to the glory and praise of God.

In Your holy and precious name,

Amen

A Prayer for Gideon
Taken from Ephesians 3:16–21

Father,

*I pray that out of Your glorious riches You may strengthen
Gideon with power through Your spirit in his inner being,
so that Christ may dwell in Gideon's heart through faith,
and I pray that Gideon being rooted and established in love,
may grasp how wide and long and high and deep is the love
of Christ and that Gideon may know this love that sur-
passes knowledge—that he may be filled to the measure of
all the fullness of God.*

*Now to Him who is able to do immeasurably more than all
we ask or imagine, to Him be glory and honor and praise
throughout this generation and every generation to come.*

Amen.

A Prayer for Gideon
Taken from Ephesians 4:25–5:2

Father,

I pray that Gideon would put off falsehoods and speak the truth. I pray that in his anger, he will not sin. I pray that his anger will be resolved promptly, not giving the devil a foothold and not allowing bitterness to grow.

I pray that Gideon will not steal. I pray that as he grows, You will develop a skill in him, that he may have something to share with those in need. I pray that no unwholesome talk may come out of his mouth, but only that which is helpful for building others up according to their needs, that it may benefit those who listen. I pray that Gideon may be kind and compassionate, forgiving those who hurt him. I pray that he may be an imitator of Christ and live a life of love.

Thank you for your love, Father.

In Your name I pray,

Amen

A Prayer for Gideon
Taken from Colossians 1:9–11

Father,

I thank You for Gideon. He is a gift from You. Thank You for blessing my life with him.

God, I ask that You fill Gideon with the knowledge of Your will through all spiritual wisdom and understanding. I pray that Gideon may live a life worthy of the Lord and that he may please You in every way: bearing fruit in every good work, growing in the knowledge of God, being strengthened with all power according to Your glorious might so that Gideon may have great endurance, great patience, and joyfully give thanks to You and honor Your holy name.

In Christ's name I pray,

Amen.

Points to Ponder:

What gives you hope?

Where do you put your hope (doctors, therapists, spouse, the Lord)?

How do you think the power of prayer could change your heart and your child's life?

Through these scripture passages, have you learned anything new or different about the character of God?

Memorize Lamentations 3:21–25

Part III

The Journey

CHAPTER SEVEN

On Grief

Grief is a process. It is one thing I lump into the "necessary evil" category. To be whole and healed, to love and feel loved, grief is a journey we must all walk. If we refuse to move, we only condemn our families and ourselves, trading everything we hold dear for anger or depression, stuck in stale survival. That is not living.

Grief has been summarized in five basic steps: Denial, Anger, Depression, Bargaining, and Acceptance. Guilt is not a typical stage of grief. However, I find an exception when a parent is grieving a loss in regards to their child. In reading books on parents grieving the deaths of their children, I found that all of them struggled with guilt. So we will deal with this guilt as a stage of our grief. The four stages of grief we will center our attention on are Denial, Anger, Guilt, and Acceptance.

Let's analyze the example from Chapter Four of the teething toy. Keep in mind here, a lot of grief transpires

over the period of months and years. For the sake of a con-
cise example, I am using a situation that unfolded over the
course of two days.

Shock is what we were feeling when presented with the
idea of tying tubing around Gideon so he could have something to bite on. Shock gives you time to process what is
happening; it is an absolute stop time. Adam's initial response was that Gideon was fine, and we did not need to
regress in his development. We could call this denial. Denial is a prolonged state of shock.

At first Adam did not even want to discuss the situation,
this is typical of denial. The thinking is that there is no problem, therefore there is nothing to discuss. Prayerfully and
gently, I continued to pursue this issue with him. We walked
through denial and into the anger and guilt stages (again
this wasn't a life-changing trauma; it was just a toy). In the
midst of the anger stage, we felt frustration for having to buy
an infant toy for our three-year-old son. The frustration was
not about our son at all. The toy was one more thing re-
minding us that life at our house was not normal; it was not
easy, and sometimes it seemed totally unfair.

I felt embarrassed. I felt that our little boy might be
looked down upon because he had a teething toy or that
we might be condemned for giving it to him. I immediately
felt guilt, examining his infant stage for critical errors I might
have made. I nursed for a year. He had teething toys and
plenty of other things to bite and chew. He wouldn't take a
pacifier, but there was one in his room if he had wanted it.
I did everything that I thought was the best for Gideon;
this delay was not my fault. We talked through our feelings

and were able to move to acceptance. We went to the store, bought the toy, and used it to enable our son's progress.

The following is an article written by Phil Rich, Ed.D., MSW. The article is specifically about grieving the death of a loved one, however, I found that it parallels quite amazingly to what we are discussing here. Grief is grief. The article is entitled *The Grief Continuum: Three Stages of Grief Work*, and it has been printed here with permission from the publisher and the author. The original source came from *WWW.SelfHelpMagazine.Com*

He writes:

> *Grief is an inevitable part of life. For some, it's a relatively quick journey lasting a few months; for others, a journey that may take years to complete. This process of working through grief is frequently referred to as "grief work."*

The Grief Continuum

> *Although the grief experience is intensely personal, there are some fairly typical stages of [grief]. These range from initial shock, to anguish and despair once the realization of the loss sinks in, to eventual acceptance. Within each stage are specific emotional and psychological tasks which must be worked through completely before people can move on to successfully complete the tasks of the next stage.*

> *Although these stages are generally a predictable part of the mourning process, grief doesn't always move in a straight line. The stages tend to flow together and fluctuate, so it's not always possible to tell which stage people are in. Emotions*

see-saw, and overwhelming feelings pass and then return. Moods wash in and out like the tide. Just when people think they are "over" it, a sound, smell, or image can send them back into emotional turmoil. This back and forth movement may occur over a period of months, or even years.

Although varying from person to person, it's not unusual for the active stages of grieving to last 1–2 full years or more. But understanding the stages of grief can also help the [person] see that they aren't alone in their confusion, turmoil, and pain, and that things improve as they progress through the stages. It can also help people aid to complete the necessary grief work, which includes:

- facing the reality of loss
- working through painful memories
- experiencing the full range of emotions associated with loss
- coping with the situational and lifestyle changes resulting from the loss
- adapting to the loss, and reconfiguring their own life

The Stages of Grief

The goal of grief work is not to find ways to avoid or by-pass the emotional turmoil and upsets brought by loss. Instead, its goals involve working through the tasks and emotions of each stage of grief.

Stage 1: "Acclamation and Adjustment." In this first stage, the tasks largely involve dealing with the initial emotional shock and disorientation often brought by [the loss]:

- *Adjusting to changes brought by the loss*
- *Functioning appropriately in daily life*
- *Keeping emotions and behaviors in check*
- *Accepting support*

Stage 2: "Emotional Immersion and Deconstruction." Although the initial impact of the [loss] has passed, emotions are often deeply felt during this stage. The [person grieving must] face and have to deal with the changes that the [loss] has brought, and often challenges to their beliefs about the way things should be. This stage incorporates the most active aspects of grief work. It's not that this stage is any more intense than the first stage—in fact, it's difficult to imagine that anything could be more intense than the period immediately following a loss. But during this stage, people are likely to become deeply immersed in their feelings, and very internally-focused. It's also quite common for the [person] to undergo a "deconstruction" of their values and beliefs, as they question why [this has happened]. The tasks associated with Stage 2 include:

- *Contending with reality*
- *Development of insight*
- *Reconstructing personal values and beliefs*
- *Acceptance and letting go*

Stage 3: "Reclamation and Reconciliation." In this final stage many issues about the [loss] have been resolved, and the [one grieving will] more fully begin to reclaim and move on with their lives. This stage is generally thought to be one marked by "recovery" from grief. But [this significant loss] leaves a permanent mark on people's lives in the sense that things can't be restored to the way they were before [this happened]. However, people can begin to rebuild, creating a new life for themselves and re-engaging with the world around them. As this stage ends, the [person grieving will] become reconciled to the [loss] itself, and the changes it's brought to their lives. Perhaps most important, they begin to live in the present, rather than the past, re-establish who they are in the world, and plan a future. The primary tasks of this stage are:

- *Development of social relations*
- *Decisions about changes in life style*
- *Renewal of self-awareness*
- *Acceptance of responsibility*

Respecting Loss and Grief

Talking about "recovering" from grief is almost disrespectful, as life is never restored to the way it was before [this kind of significant loss]. When people talk of recovery, they really refer to overcoming grief and adapting to life after the [loss]. This is an important distinction to draw, because the purpose of grief work is not to "get over" loss, but to adjust to its consequences, and restore balance.

What incredible insight Rich gives to our grief! It is so liberating to understand that I don't have to "get over" the fact that my son has special needs. The purpose of this grief work is to adjust to the consequences and restore balance in my heart and my home.

I have a friend named Donna who is one fellow traveler on this journey. In an e-mail about grief, she wrote, "Sev-

eral months before we got Shayna's diagnosis, I was in denial. I was hoping that it really wasn't autism. And once we got the diagnosis I thought I would feel some relief knowing what was wrong with her. But, instead, it felt like we went over this little hill just to find out that we were facing this new huge mountain which we had no idea how to get over. The autism diagnosis presented us with all these new issues and decisions and needs to learn and deal with all the problems that go with it. It's just plain overwhelming and your own emotional well being all too easily gets ignored along with other things."

Have you ever felt like you crossed a hill only to find a mountain? Her words clearly depict what we all face when we face the diagnosis. The grief we encounter seems insurmountable. However, we have this assurance from God's Word: *In all these things we are more than conquerors through him who loved us. For I am convinced that neither death nor life, neither angels nor demon, neither the present nor the future, nor any powers, neither height nor depth, nor anything else in all creation, will be able to separate us from the love of God that is in Christ Jesus our Lord.* (Romans 8:37–39)

The following four chapters take each stage of grief to discuss its meaning and purpose. Denial is the initial numbness that enables us to function amidst the chaos. Anger gives us the ability to ask questions, state our protest (regardless of how futile it may be), and seek out the cause or responsible person for the injustice. Guilt is how we make sense of that which makes no sense at all. I wish I could claim that as an original thought, but it is just a regurgitated insight into grief. Guilt is taking the responsibility on as our own. Acceptance is a refreshing wave of resolution. It is how we move past the madness and into peace and purpose. Let's walk this together.

Points to Ponder:

How do you feel as you stand on the threshold of embracing this grief process?

How has denial, anger, and guilt presented itself in your life to this point?

What do you think it will take for you to 'adjust to the consequences' of having a child with special needs?

What do you think it will take for you to 'restore balance' in your live and in your home?

Memorize Romans 8:37–39

CHAPTER EIGHT

Not My Child ... (Denial)

As I previously wrote, the summer our son turned three, he was diagnosed as developmentally disabled. What a shattering thought! The cracks in my reality were becoming exceedingly apparent. "Disabled? He walks. He talks (in his own way). He laughs. He plays. What is disabled about him?" I questioned. "Sure, he doesn't do things some of the other boys his age are doing—and yeah, he still does some things the other kids have grown out of, but every child is different!"

We had received this enormous, all encompassing label: developmentally disabled. There was no real meaning behind it; it was just stuck to him so that he could receive the help he needed through the school district. It gave us no direction, no insight. They just attached this label and sent him on his way.

When Gideon was three and a half, we made an appointment for him to see a developmental specialist to be tested for specific developmental disorders. The process of making the appointment was one that took many months. I had received the phone number for a well-respected specialist that worked through the children's hospital in our state. Apprehensively, I called. They sent an initial intake form, and it took me four months to send it back. There was so much grief to walk through.

During that four-month period, I battled so much denial. At times I convinced myself that Gideon was going to be just fine without any further help. I decided that all of this was something he would just out-grow over time—I mean, at some point he's going to be able to differentiate between a boy and a girl, right? I had reasoned that I was blowing this up, making it bigger than it really was. I decided that his problems were not as 'bad' as I had made them out to be.

One night, as we sat in our small group Bible study from church, my heart just came bursting open as I confessed all that was going on with Gideon. The pain erupted from within me; at one point I wept so deeply that I could not even speak. The reality was staring me in the face; I could reject it no longer. The denial had been shattered, and those broken pieces were no longer capable of restraining me.

I did send the intake form to the specialist, and we heard an immediate response. Gideon needed to be evaluated. His delays indicated something more than just the typical developmental problems. As we waited for his appointment to arrive, I wrestled with what the outcome of the assessment would be.

Through this time of waiting I felt the Lord drawing me close, challenging me to trust Him with 'whatever' . . . whatever the diagnosis . . . whatever the treatment . . . whatever the cost, emotionally, physically, and financially. Would I trust Him? Part of trusting Him, I realized, was saying that I would accept His will—whatever that will would be. For me, this was an amazing lesson in healing.

Several people encouraged us to take Gideon to the elders in our church and pray for his healing. James 5:14–15 says, *Is anyone among you sick? Let him call for the elders of the church, and let them pray over him, anointing him with oil in the name of the Lord. And the prayer of faith will save the sick, and the Lord will raise him up.*

I wrestled with this for quite some time. My questioning was this: if God was going to heal Gideon, then God would heal him. My pleading was not going to change His mind; He is sovereign. If God is not going to heal Gideon, then why should I put my hope in healing so that my heart is crushed when it does not happen? Well, I found that my perspective was really wrong! I had taken my hope from the Lord, and I had put my hope in 'healing.' Another error that I made was in my definition of healing. An older, much wiser friend shared with me that healing comes in many different forms.

I remember, as a little girl, watching most of the people in our church gather around my mom, one Sunday morning. Her cancer was terminal; she was dying. I watched them praying, pleading for her healing. Though I only remember this one specific time, my father said there were many, many such occasions. In the end, my mom died. Did God say, "No!"? Did God refuse to heal her? Did God turn a deaf ear to their pleading?

Healing comes in many ways; my friend was so right on! God did heal her. God healed her heart. She became a testimony of God's faithfulness. Her death left countless ripples in the hearts of all who heard about her life. She walked courageously, in the face of immense pain, every day of her life. She trusted her husband, her children, and her ministries into the hands of her Father. She died a hero's death, and that death was her ultimate healing. My father shared this insight: if she had been healed physically, she would have still faced death. In her death, she was free and completely whole; in her death, she was healed.

I caught myself in the trap of believing that healing is some supernatural, instantaneous, radically life altering, distinct, solitary event. Healing comes in many ways; many times healing is a process.

My much wiser friend speaks from personal experience. She has a son in his thirties who is a quadriplegic. Gary has Cerebral Palsy. His mental capacities are strong; he is a very intelligent man. However, he is severely physically handi-capped. My friend prayed daily for her son's healing. Gary also prayed for his healing, and God has healed him. Gary will live every day of his life in a wheel chair, yet he is very secure in the healing that he has received from God. The Lord has touched Gary's heart in a remarkable way. Gary now says, with joy, that he is so thankful for his Cerebral Palsy. He is able to minister to people that he never would have without the disability. He is grateful for his handicap! Gary knows that life is temporary, and for this life, he rides in a wheel chair. Gary also knows that Heaven is forever, and when he gets there, he will have a strong, whole body. God has healed Gary. There is no doubt of that!

*Romans 8:28 says, And we know that all things work to-
gether for good to those who love God . . .*

As mentioned in chapter five, my good friend Wendy
has a quadriplegic father and paraplegic brother. In Wendy's
own words, she clearly describes the healing that God works
and how amazing His ways are:

*My dad broke his neck at age twenty. I believe that God
allowed there to be a consequence to his behavior—he dove
into a sandpit filled with water and hit his forehead on a
ledge which broke his neck. The consequence of this action
was paralysis. If this accident never happened he may have
gone a completely different direction in life. He is an amazing man!*

*As a result of this accident—good came out of it. The major
thing was that he became a Christian. After my dad's accident, many people said to him that if only he had enough
faith he could be healed (I thank God my dad didn't completely lose his faith because of over zealous Christians!).
God decided not to heal my dad (physically). Yet God pre-
formed many miracles along the way . . .*

*Most of the quadriplegics, during that time, only lived very
short lives—my dad has lived forty years in that chair! My
dad had a fulltime job for thirty-two years helping others
with disabilities get jobs and the help they needed to live
successful lives. My dad has made a huge impact on those
around him, despite his own physical limitations. I believe
he is a different man because of this tragedy. Good has come
from bad.*

Another good/bad thing was that he was unable to have children, and therefore they adopted my brother and me. My brother had a second chance when he was three and a half to have a family (He was in foster homes before then). He may not have ever been adopted into a loving home because of his disability. My parents wanted a special needs child, because they felt that they could give a child a good home. Because my mom is a nurse she could care for his physical needs. My dad could relate with him about his disability. It amazes me the strength and love my parents both have. I know that they are special people. God gave me a second chance for a healthy family too. I thank God that things happened the way they did. I am not happy my dad is in a wheelchair, but I am happy he is my dad! I don't understand God's way, but God did make good out of the bad.

What incredible testimonies of God's goodness in the midst of tragedy!

Healing did come for Gideon too. As usual, it did not happen in the way that I expected it, once again proving God's sovereignty. When Gideon began with treatment for the Celiac Disease, the developmental problems began to dissipate. Gideon was more than a year delayed in much of his cognitive development and speech. He had significant behavioral issues as well, but we were not able to determine if they were related to the physical or developmental problems.

Treatment for the Celiac Disease is life-long adherence to an intense gluten-free diet. This is the only way to stop the progression of the disease. When he began on the Celiac diet, we prayed that it would heal his gastrointestinal problems, but it also began to resolve the developmental and behavioral issues. After he had been on the diet for a few months, I told his pediatrician, "You know, we actually have a calm, gentle, timid child. This is the first time in four years I have been able to see this beautiful side of Gideon."

We do not fully understood how or why Celiac Disease has such an enormous effect on behavior and development; studies are being conducted to find the link. His body fought so hard and so long just to keep going; we believe it had no extra recourses to put towards development. Celiac Disease is for life, and we still struggle at times with the health and learning issues. However, God has healed Gideon and will continue to work healing in Gideon's life. He will never be whole in this body (unless God decides to change that). We know that Celiac Disease is for this life only; Gideon will receive a complete healing when Jesus brings him home to Heaven.

My healing began after I laid down all of my questions, all of my fears, and all of my hopelessness at the feet of Christ. The first step was breaking through the denial. There is not much that can be said about denial except that it is. It is what allows us to function when the emotional toll is too costly. At some point we must embrace the pain and jump in. In the depth of this, we must be willing to trust God. He is the only one who is capable to guide us through all the grief. He is the healer: the healer of our hearts, the healer of our souls, the healer of our lives. We just have to resolve to rest in the fact that no matter how He chooses to work in our lives we will trust Him and walk with Him.

Points to Ponder:

Have you walked through your denial?
What caused the cracking of your denial?
How do you feel about healing?
What type of healing has God worked in your life?
In your child's life?
Memorize Romans 8:28

CHAPTER NINE

Mad at the World (Anger)

When we step out of the anger and view it as objectively as possible, we understand that anger is a part of this grief process.

I rested in the peace that 'God purposed this for my life.' It was a gentle way for me to make sense of the madness. But when the anger hit, I realized that by saying, "God purposed this . . .", I was actually blaming God. I was saying, "God, YOU DID THIS TO ME! YOU CREATED MY SON THIS WAY!" I was angry!

It was in that anger that I found such a peace from the Lord. I sat in quietness, one morning. My prayers had become too painful, too questioning. I thought of how God had answered Job when he questioned Him. Job 38–41 give His words of rebuke. But I did not feel rebuke from the Lord that morning. I felt a gentle, yet strong comfort sweep through my soul.

God is not intimidated by my questions. He is not threatened by my insecurities. His power is infinite. My anger could never rob Him of His omnipotence. In my heartache and pain, in my anger and confusion, I blamed God. I needed someone or something to set my anger against. God was the safest place that I found to do just that.

I found that God did not strike me with wrath for my searching, but instead met me in the midst of my hurt. I love the New King James Version of Jeremiah 29:11–13, *"For I know the thoughts that I think toward you," says the Lord, "thoughts of peace and not of evil, to give you a future and a hope. Then you will call upon Me and go and pray to Me, and I will listen to you. And you will seek Me and find Me, when you search for Me with all your heart."*

With all of my heart, though desperately hurting, I was seeking truth. I found the truth. God used my dear friends, Kevin and Wendy, to speak the truth into my heart. It was as if all that I had known had slipped away. The anger consumed me. God used these friends to speak the truth back into the midst of my situation, into the midst of my pain. I read my friend's words and thought, "But I know all of this stuff . . ." The fact was that even though I 'knew' it, I had let the anger stand in my way of understanding how it applied in this situation, to this pain.

Within the safety of a dear friendship, I confided my anger and hurt. They knew I was not in danger but understood I was desperate for my ground to be stabilized with some encouragement and reminders of God's character. Kevin's words were so powerful, insightful, and timely. I thought it best if you read it directly from him. He wrote,

I believe that God's work is perfect, and that any flaws we see are the result of a broken world. I believe that God has

set natural and physical laws in place to govern the concrete universe, as we know it. These laws have been bent and corrupted by sin. Sin "broke" the world we live in. So, Gideon's body is now bearing the consequences of existing in a broken world. The only way for God to fix this broken world is to remove all the sin. The only way to remove the sin is to remove human ability to choose. If God removes our ability to choose, then we all become robots and we loose our ability to have relationship. Since we were created to have relationship with God, we would be incapable of the very purpose we were created for. So, God cannot "fix" the world without taking away our purpose for existing.

As far as we can understand, God is not healing Gideon yet. I don't know why God is not healing him yet. We may never know why. But we need to remember that (1) God can heal him and (2) God may still heal him and (3) if God does not heal him, He will at least use it for some sort of good, because that is what He does. God will do whatever He will do. If we pray for God to heal Gideon, our prayers will not obligate God to heal Gideon. However, our prayers may allow Him to do it sooner for spiritual reasons beyond our understanding. However, praying can only help . . . it certainly will not hurt. If nothing else, prayer is time with God and brings us closer to God.

God does not always allow things for a reason. Sometimes God allows things because He cannot change them without "fixing" the broken world. God is not ready to fix the broken world yet. There is a certain level of chaos that He must allow running wild because removing the chaos would *mean removing free choice for people. Satan has a certain level of freedom to cause trouble. However, we are promised that God will work things out for the good of those who love Him. (Romans 8:28)*

But here's the key . . . Even if not in this life, it will be right in the next. Someday Gideon will eat birthday cake and grilled chicken and prime rib and Grandpa Gabriel's homemade angel bread . . . and Gideon will run as fast as any other person . . . and Gideon will understand and comprehend God's creation just as well as any other person . . . and Gideon will not only know the difference between male and female, but he will know the deepest, most profound mysteries of an infinite God because Gideon will be with God in Heaven in a perfect body that is uncorrupted by a sinful, broken world!

It's okay to desire the pain and the trouble to be removed. Let God decide whether or not He will remove it. Be ready to accept it if He does not. But don't ever quit asking Him to remove it because you know He will only remove it if His wisdom says it's okay to remove it. Ask for what you want, and let His "yes" or "no" be yes or no.

The main thing I'm trying to say is that God can handle your prayers. Be honest with God. Don't stop praying because (you fear that) you may pray the wrong thing. Also, try to keep an "eternal" perspective. Gideon may have a rough life, but it will only be for this life and not for eternity. I know that does not make it better, but it may help you to cope. When you get really discouraged, imagine Gideon someday in heaven having a blast! Again, it does not solve the problem, but it is one of the better coping strategies that we have.

I was very grateful for Kevin's wise words. He reaffirmed what I knew to be true and reminded me of God's goodness. This enabled me to move forward as I walked through the anger. Facing the question of 'did God cause this or did God allow this?' was part of my journey.

The marriage and family therapist at our home church, stated that the issue of 'did God cause this or did God allow this?' is one of the deepest, most difficult, soul-searching issues that we face as Christians. He went on to say that we might not ever know the answer to that question here on earth. However, in the midst of the pain that caused that soul searching, we must, instead, ask ourselves this question: Is God trust-worthy? Can I trust God through this chaos, this madness, this consuming, drenching, drowning storm? The answer is YES! Though everything in our world is in a constant state of change, one thing that will never change is God. He is constant. *He is the same yesterday, today, and forever* (Hebrews 13:8).

He is worthy of our trust because he is our Father; John 1:12–13 says, *Yet to all who received him, to those who believed in His name, He gave the right to become children of God—children born not of natural descent, nor of human decision or a husband's will, but born of God.* Isaiah 63:16 says, *You, O Lord, are our Father; our Redeemer from Everlasting is Your name.*

He is worthy of our trust because he is faithful; Deuteronomy 7:9 says, *Therefore know that the Lord your God, He is God, the faithful God who keeps covenant and mercy for a thousand generations with those who love Him and keep His commandments.*

He is worthy of our trust because He is holy; Isaiah 6:3 says, *Holy, holy, holy is the Lord of hosts; the whole earth is full of His glory!*

He is compassionate and full of mercy. *Indeed we count them blessed who endure. You have heard of the perseverance of Job and seen the end intended by the Lord—that the Lord is very compassionate and merciful* (James 5:11).

He is patient, kind, humble, gentle, giving; He never fails. He is all of the things that 1 Corinthians 13 describes love to be, because *God is love* (1 John 4:8).

We know we can trust Him, but we still need to deal with the anger that we feel. Anger is a part of this grief process. Anger is necessary. Anger is a God-given emotion. I once heard that anger is one emotion that *gives* us energy. Depression, sorrow, and the like seem to drain energy from us. Anger actually stimulates the adrenaline and gives us determination and drive to fight for the injustice we feel.

The Bible says in Psalm 4 verse 4, *Be angry, and sin not.* Another translation says, *In your anger do not sin.* The Bible never tells us not to be angry. It says, "Be angry"! But it warns us that in our anger we are not to sin.

We can use our anger, the adrenaline drive, for our good and the good of those around us, or we can use it for our harm and hurt those whom we love. Every day we read in the paper or hear on the news about someone using their anger to hurt themselves or someone else. This is so destructive and just compounds the problem. However, there are many examples of people using their anger for good; it just rarely makes the headlines.

Patricia Pena is a woman who has used her anger to aid in her healing and the healing of many others. She is using her anger to fight for education and legislation against the use of cell phones while driving. Here is her story:

Two-year-old Morgan was a happy little girl, the pride of her parents. One morning Morgan and her mom, Patricia, were in the car heading home. As they drove, Morgan cheerfully sang in her car seat. Suddenly the singing stopped. The Pena's car had been broadsided at forty-five miles an hour by a man who missed a stop sign because he was dialing on his cell phone. Morgan's head injuries were too severe for her life to be saved. It might have been a blessing if she had died instantly; instead, her mother watched as life slowly drained from her little body.

Heaping insult onto injury, the man who struck and killed little Morgan Pena was fined fifty dollars and given two traffic citations. The grieving Penas were informed that there were no laws that applied to his negligence for using a cell phone while driving.

Patricia Pena has made it her crusade to educate cell phone users. She is also working with a Senator to pass legislation against cell phone abuse. I applaud this mother for using her anger to help people. Instead of turning her anger inward and allowing it to destroy her, she is using her anger for good.

We have the same option given to us. Using our anger for good does not necessarily mean that we become a politician or that we begin a crusade. However, the choice is ours: do we allow our anger to destroy us or do we use our anger to facilitate our healing and possibly help others who are in the midst of the same pain?

Points to Ponder:

Are you angry now or have you felt anger because of
your child's needs?

Who or what is your anger directed at?

What positive steps of action can you take to use your
anger for good?

Is God worthy of your trust?

List 5–10 characteristics that affirm God's worth of trust
in your life.

Memorize Psalm 4:4

CHAPTER TEN

No One Else to Blame (Guilt)

My grandmother was a beautiful woman with intense strength. She survived a childhood that was, at times, not very pleasant. She fell in love with a medic fighting in World War II and married him shortly after his return home. Her first born child, a daughter, had polio. Her second born child, a son, had his first heart attack at age two. Her third child, a son, died of leukemia when he was two years old. Her fourth child, my mother, was born shortly after the death of Timmy. Who could rejoice in the birth of a child in the midst of immense sorrow? Then after thirty-three short years, my mother was gone. Between the births of her fourth and fifth child, my grandmother had four miscarriages. Three years after losing her daughter, she lost her husband of nearly fifty years. She was an amazing woman of prayer, a devout Catholic, deeply devoted to her family, and she loved God. I believe He was what gave her the strength to hang on.

My Grandmother carried this sense of responsibility with her until the day she died. I had a long visit with her just before she passed away. Still clinging to the responsibility of her family, she confided, "I feel like I'm ruining everyone's Christmas!"

"Grandma," I gently answered, "You don't have to worry about us. We are going to be okay." She held on until Christmas Day; I believe she just ran out of strength.

One thing she carried to her grave was her own feelings of guilt. Her daughter had polio; how could that have possibly been her fault? Her son had heart disease. She was not to blame. Another son died so dreadfully young; he had cancer. How was that her doing? My own mother died of breast cancer, and she took the responsibility for that as well. She lost four children to miscarriage; she did nothing wrong. Yet for all of this sickness, for all of this death, she carried the silent, needless burden of guilt.

It's easy for us to look at this and admit that her guilt was unmerited, the weight of it, agonizing. However, if we do a deep inventory of our own soul, I would venture to guess that most, if not all of us, feel or have felt guilt for our child's special needs.

In my own need to make sense of the madness, I decided that all of Gideon's problems were my fault! For the first two years of Gideon's life, I felt the great oppression of my own guilt. This is how I broke it down: The gastrointestinal problems started with the first diagnosis of Reflux Disease. He developed Reflux because he was born three weeks early. He was born three weeks early because he went into fetal distress. He went into fetal distress because I was induced. I was induced because I developed pre-eclampsia.

I developed pre-eclampsia because of my ambivalence about pregnancy and my fear of motherhood.

I needed an explanation, and this was the way I could make sense of it. If I blamed myself, then at least I understood why this was happening. I created this chain of events that, in reality, didn't fit together all that well.

The first step in dealing with our guilt is admitting and expressing our guilt. I sat down with a Christian counselor, and over four or five sessions, we discussed the trauma of Gideon's birth and what life had become since his birth. This compassionate mother, an experienced counselor, looked me in the eyes and said, "Rebeckah, this is not your fault!"

I was so confused by her words. At that time, I didn't even realize that my guilt was irrational. My only response was to shake my head in disbelief.

The next step in dealing with our guilt is understanding the reality of what is actually going on. My guilt stemmed from the pregnancy and birth experience. I had to do some investigation to gain acceptance of the medical complications that happened during that time. I also had to view each link in the guilt chain through the light of reality.

A baby is considered full-term at thirty-seven weeks; it is highly unlikely that Gideon's gastrointestinal problems stemmed from a slightly early delivery. There are many premature babies born without significant long-term health problems. There was no reality in my linking these together. A pregnant mom cannot force herself to develop pre-eclampsia. The anxiety over motherhood and the ambivalence of an 'unplanned' pregnancy are very typical! My obstetrician's nurse reassured me that I was feeling the same emotions that many moms face with their first pregnancy.

I had several ultrasounds through my second and third trimesters because I bled throughout the pregnancy. During weeks thirty-five and thirty-six, I had a very sudden and large weight gain and my blood pressure had risen significantly. I had proteinuria (the presence of protein in the urine), and I was admitted to the hospital after expressing concern over some visual disturbances I was experiencing. The reality of this is that a complication to my pregnancy developed without any fault of my own.

My doctor did what he saw best fit for my well being and the well being of my unborn child. Because of the severity of my asthma, they were unable to use cervical gel to help the natural birth process along. They started me on a very slow pitocin drip. Gideon immediately went into fetal distress. His heart was experiencing severe decelerations. They helped me adjust my position in bed and the position of the fetal monitor, but nothing helped. The nursing staff was unable to reach the obstetrician, so they turned off the pitocin. Even after the drip was stopped, Gideon's heart rate did not recover. The nurse sent an urgent message that my doctor needed to come immediately, and they began prepping the operating room. The obstetrician looked at the fetal monitor printout; the late and decelerated heart activity continued. He sat down beside my bed, took my hand, and very gently explained to Adam and me that we needed to deliver the baby by cesarean. I was rushed into the operating room, and the rest is history.

Guilt is very real, but the rationalities that create our guilt are often a thinly spun web. When we allow ourselves

100

to look at our guilt through the eyes of reality, we clearly see a very different picture.

One way I overcame the guilt was to research pre-eclampsia and fetal distress. It brought me to the very humble realization that God's hand was on my life and Gideon's life through the whole terrible ordeal! As I began to understand the extreme danger that pre-eclampsia posed on my life, I was grateful for God's protection and the wisdom of my doctor. Even more astonishing was the understanding of fetal distress.

I thank God, now, every time I think about this, for the quick response and initiative of the nurse to discontinue the intravenous drip without the doctor's approval. I thank God for the obstetrician we "ended up with," for his tenderness and ability to calmly talk with us despite his understanding of the critical situation we were in. I thank God for the way He orchestrated the entire birth process; no longer did I feel guilt, rather immense gratitude! When I realized what could have been (severe brain damage or death), I fell to my face in grateful thanksgiving and praised God for His hand on our lives.

Many times we can't see the "what could have been." God allowed me, in this, to understand. For me, this resolved much of the anger and the guilt. I found that I didn't need someone to blame. This was a real perspective-grabber for me. I didn't need to find the person or the thing responsible for the injustice. I didn't need to create a web of guilt to trap myself in. Rather, I realized, God knew what was happening; He knew that there was a mother with a pregnancy complication and a baby with physical and developmental problems. He didn't reach down and stop what was happening. However, in His amazing love, He did choose to protect Gideon and protect me.

When we analyze our guilt, we are faced with the reality of its cause. Our definition of guilt was "making sense of that which makes no sense at all," and for most of us, our guilt is, honestly, unrealistic. The events that led us to this place are not our fault. However, for some, the events that drew you here are the result of your own choices.

Some consequences of choices are simply the natural order of things that require us to deal with life, resulting from our own action. Wendy's father was in a diving accident at the age of twenty; he has lived for forty years in a wheel chair. This was a natural consequence to his actions. He chose to dive into that sandpit; his head hit the ledge on his way down. Of course, he did not intend to break his neck or become paralyzed, but instead of sitting in a heap of self-pity, he chose to use this tragedy for his good and for the good of others.

Some choices we make are damaging, and we need to take responsibility for the consequences of our action or inaction because healing can only come when we face the situation with truth. Our choices don't stop with one bad decision or tragedy. Through the pain, we must continue to choose. As that old saying goes: "we can choose to make our lives better, or we can choose to become bitter." We can choose to pursue health and wholeness, or we can choose death.

When damage occurs due to our choices, we must take responsibility. When I think about responsibility, blame, and guilt, the passage in Romans 8 continually comes to mind.

Therefore, there is now no condemnation for those who are in Christ Jesus, because through Christ Jesus the law of the Spirit of life set me free from the law of sin and death. For what the law was powerless to do in that it was weakened by the sinful nature, God did by sending his own Son in the likeness of sinful man to be a sin offering. And so he condemned sin in sinful man, in order that the righteous requirements of the law might be fully met in us, who do not live according to the sinful nature but according to the Spirit. Those who live according to the sinful nature have their minds set on what that nature desires, but those who live in accordance with the Spirit have their minds set on what the Spirit desires. The mind of sinful man is death, but the mind controlled by the Spirit is life and peace; the sinful mind is hostile to God. It does not submit to God's law, nor can it do so. Those controlled by the sinful nature cannot please God.

There is forgiveness and freedom. It is found in Christ. If you are struggling, today, with the feelings of guilt or condemnation for the choices you have made, I encourage you to seek our Father. Confess your fears, your guilt, and the silent burden you carry. Know that *If we confess our sins, He is faithful and just and will forgive us our sins and purify us from all unrighteousness* (1 John 1:9).

Points to Ponder:

Do you feel guilt over your child's special needs?

Where does your guilt stem from?

Is your guilt justified?

What practical steps can you take to find the reality for that which causes your guilt?

Memorize Romans 8:1 and 1 John 1:9

CHAPTER ELEVEN

Acceptance

We defined acceptance as a refreshing wave of resolution. One aspect of acceptance is realizing the point where we can help and the point where we need to let it go. From the time Gideon turned two and entered the Birth to Three Program to the time he turned four and received his Celiac diagnosis, I was more than a mom. I was a doctor researching gastrointestinal disorders and Pervasive Developmental Disorders. I read every article that I could find on the World Wide Web; I read every book that our local library had. I was a speech therapist. When Gideon had difficulty with recall, I would model speech. When he had difficulty with speech sounds, I would sit down and have him watch the form and movement of my tongue and lips. I was an early childhood teacher. We would drill colors, shapes, gender, numbers, and letters. We worked on drawing and cutting. We buttoned and laced and zipped and snapped.

I was so weary from this 'Super Mom' routine. I was filled with despair as I realized where we needed to be and understood where we were. I was frustrated as I thought of how much we had worked, and how little progress had been made.

Finally one day Gideon's teacher told me to stop. She told me to stop reading about development because no matter how much I read, it was not going to change Gideon. She told me to stop working on speech with him because he will learn from me by listening to conversation. She told me to stop drilling concepts and fine motor skills because he will learn it when he is ready.

"Then what do I do?" I asked.

"You be his mom!" She replied. "You *love* him. You *enjoy* him. You be his mom, and **that's all**."

What an amazing gift she had given me. She gave me the empowerment to just play with him without finding something therapeutic in our time together. She gave me permission to let the doctors do their jobs and the therapists do their jobs. She encouraged me to allow the teachers to do their jobs, and me to do mine.

Part of acceptance, for me, was accepting my role in Gideon's life. I cannot do it all. I need the doctors, therapists, and teachers. I need the babysitter to give me an afternoon away, and it's not admitting weakness to say that I need a break. I need the lady from church who thinks it's fun to experiment with foods that fit into his special diet because not all of my creations are edible. I need the little boy down the street who thinks Gideon is a great friend because he fills a need that I could never meet. I am Gideon's mom, and that's all I need to be. I am grateful for the growth that this grief work has produced in my life, but it has not been without considerable pain.

A friend emailed me the following story; the source is unknown:

There was a group of women in a Bible study on the book of Malachi. As they were studying Chapter Three, they came across Verse Three which says: "He will sit as a refiner and purifier of silver."

This verse puzzled the women and they wondered what this statement meant about the character and nature of God. One of the women offered to find out about the process of refining silver and get back to the group at their next Bible study session.

That week this woman called up a silversmith and made an appointment to watch him at work. She didn't mention anything about the reason for her interest in silver beyond her curiosity about the process of refining silver.

As she watched the silver smith, he held a piece of silver over the fire and let it heat up. He explained that in refining silver, one needed to hold the silver in the middle of the fire where the flames were hottest so as to burn away all the impurities.

The woman thought about God holding us in such a hot spot then she thought again about the verse, that says, "He sits as a refiner and purifier of silver."

She asked the silversmith if it was true that he had to sit there in front of the fire the whole time the silver was being refined.

The man answered that yes, he not only had to sit there holding the silver, but he had to keep his eyes on the silver the entire time it was in the fire. For if the silver was left even a moment too long in the flames, it would be destroyed.

The woman was silent for a moment. Then she asked the silversmith, how do you know when the silver is fully refined?

He smiled at her and answered, "Oh, that's the easy part. When I see my image reflected in it."

That truly states what this process of grief has done in my own heart. I have felt those hot flames lick me, almost dancing in laughter around me, challenging me to give up and be consumed. Rather, the Father has held me close with a watchful eye, giving respite and reprieve before I surrendered to the flames. My journey through this grief is not about my own strength, but, rather, the goodness of God, the quality of His character, and the completeness of His love.

Sara Groves wrote one song that is very dear to my heart. It is entitled, "He's Always Been Faithful"

Morning by morning I wake up to find the power and comfort of God's hand in mine. Season by season I watch Him amazed, in awe of the mystery of His perfect ways. All I

*have need of His hand will provide. He's always been faith-
ful to me.*

*I can't remember a trial or a pain He did not recycle to
bring me gain. I can't remember one single regret in serv-
ing God only and trusting His hand. All I have need of His
hand will provide. He's always been faithful to me.*

*This is my anthem. This is my song, the theme of the
stories I've heard for so long. God has been faithful, He
will be again. His loving compassion, it knows no end.
All I have need of His hand will provide. He's always
been faithful. He's always been faithful. He's always been
faithful to me.*

Another aspect of acceptance is moving past the madness and walking into peace and purpose. Listen to a
mother's words about her special child:

*I am often asked to describe the experience of raising a
child with a disability—to try to help people who have not
shared that unique experience to understand it, to imagine
how it would feel. It's like this . . .*

*When you're going to have a baby, it's like planning a fabu-
lous vacation trip—to Italy. You buy a bunch of guidebooks
and make wonderful plans. The Coliseum. The Michelangelo
David. The gondolas in Venice. You may learn some handy
phrases in Italian. It's all very exciting.*

*After months of eager anticipation, the day finally arrives.
You pack your bags and off you go. Several hours later, the*

plane lands. The stewardess comes in and says, "Welcome to Holland."

"Holland??!" you say. "What do you mean, Holland?? I signed up for Italy! I'm supposed to be in Italy. All my life I've dreamed of going to Italy."

But there's been a change in the flight plan. They've landed in Holland and there you must stay. The important thing is that they haven't taken you to a horrible, disgusting, filthy place, full of pestilence, famine and disease. It's just a different place.

So you must go out and buy new guidebooks. And you must learn a whole new language. And you will meet a whole new group of people you would never have met.

It's just a different place. It's slower paced than Italy, less flashy than Italy. But after you've been there for a while you catch your breath, you look around . . . and you begin to notice that Holland has windmills . . . and Holland has tulips. Holland even has Rembrandts.

But everyone you know is busy coming and going from Italy . . . and they're all bragging about what a wonderful time they had there. And for the rest of your life, you will say, "Yes, that's where I was supposed to go. That's what I had planned."

And the pain of that will never, ever, ever, ever go away . . . Because the loss of that dream is a very, very significant loss.

But . . . if you spend your life mourning the fact that you didn't get to Italy, you may never be free to enjoy the very special, the very lovely things . . . about Holland.

What a clear depiction of acceptance, of the "refreshing wave of resolution". This mother realized the truth that we all need to realize: our child's disability is not bad—it's just different. Yes, it hurts an enormous amount. It's okay to hurt, but we need to move past the enormity of this pain, by walking through the process of grief, so that we can be whole and healed, so that we can provide the love and nurture that our very special children need!

There was a three-year-old boy in my son's Early Childhood class who is nearly blind; we'll call him "Matthew." One morning I went to pick up Gideon, and Matthew's dad was sitting in the room when I arrived. Usually Mom picked him up, but today was a special day. Matthew's dad sat silently waiting for his son to realize he was there, but Matthew could not see his dad, so he had not yet discovered his surprise.

Finally, the teacher took each of Matthew's hands in her own and led him over to his father. She placed his hands on the strong arm of his daddy. Matthew began feeling his way towards the face of his father, not making one sound. Dad gently put his head down to meet Matthew's.

There, in quietness, they snuggled noses. Tears filled my eyes as I watched that man gently rub his cheek against the cheek of his little blind son. Matthew took his small hands and ran them gently down his daddy's face. His father smiled, and the joy he felt was so apparent.

Matthew had still not made mention that he recognized this person. Finally, Dad cupped Matthew's little face in his hands and guided him nose to nose. "Do you know who I am?" Matthew nodded his head. "Then why did you not say so?" With a tenderness that was so gentle and sincere he once again began rubbing his little cheek against the cheek of his father.

I turned my head as tears rolled down my face. This is what it means to find acceptance and resolve. It means we cherish the special times we share. It means we embrace the differences and love our children just the way they are. We love our children for who they are—not for what they can or cannot do.

My dear, older and wiser friend wrote me a note about finding joy in the midst of the challenges of raising Gary, her quadriplegic son with cerebral palsy. She wrote, *Instead of zeroing in on the loss, we attempted to find positive things in him. He liked whales, stars, and music. We went to the library, bought a small telescope and got him a dulcimer, which we discovered he was too handicapped to use. Finally he started playing the piano with one finger and one thumb. 'Let the Sunshine In' became our song. I sang and danced with Gary and tried to find positive everywhere—not always easy—but God draws good out of everything.* And we can too!

Our families are unique, and we need to find the joy and peace in the midst of the challenges. This does not mean the pain is gone. It means that we have found Stillness. We have found Peace. We have found Comfort. Christ is all of these things: our stillness, our peace, and our comfort.

God comforts us so we can then, in turn, extend comfort to others. *Praise be to the God and Father of our Lord*

Jesus Christ, the Father of compassion and the God of all comfort, who comforts us in all our troubles, so that we can comfort those in any trouble with the comfort we ourselves have received from God. For just as the sufferings of Christ flow over into our lives, so also through Christ our comfort overflows (2 Corinthians 1:3–5).

Points to Ponder:

Have you taken on that 'Super Mom' role?

What practical steps can you take to free yourself from the 'Super Mom' trap?

Have you found resolution within your own heart as you face your child's special needs?

What do you think it would require from you to find peace from the grief?

God has comforted you. How can you bring His comfort to someone else's life?

Memorize 2 Corinthians 1:3–5

CHAPTER TWELVE

Fearfully and Wonderfully Made

God is the creator and giver of life. Nothing is done by accident. I sometimes think of God like an orchestra conductor. He's not like a ballet instructor where all (or most) of the parts are moving together. He is like the conductor who has his watchful eye on the bassoon as well as the violas. He hears the piccolo and the tympani. He cues the clarinets to come in as the french horns ring out a clear, crisp melody. He introduces multiple layers of complimentary harmonies, all while keeping the individual voices in perfect balance. I may be one oboe in a symphony of a thousand, or the fifteenth chair violin, but I do not go unnoticed by the Master Musician.

In part, this chapter describes the development of life. It is my intention to communicate that it is done with skill; nothing is accidental. However, I want it to speak of the bigger picture: the fact that God cares about such minute details. He works endless wonders that are largely unknown to us. If He gives that much thought to an earthly body that

115

is merely 'dust' . . . that will last a few short years and then be blown away like the grass of the field, then how much more does he care about fashioning our souls?

In my conversations with moms, I hear that much pain, wonder, and worry stems from the development of the fetus. In an attempt to answer the 'why' question, so many of us have thought back to our pregnancy. "Did I do something wrong? Could I have done something differently?" Much guilt stems from the pregnancy. That was the case with me too. Researching fetal development was so healing to me because it forced me to see God's big picture of life. He is such a loving God. His goodness is endless! The astonishing miracle of developing life can only be orchestrated by the mighty hand of our loving Creator.

Prayerfully read through the descriptions of development, and allow God to assure you of His sovereignty. Let yourself feel the joy and pain of it all. Envision your child forming within your womb . . .

In the stillness of a dark sanctuary, the light of our Creator penetrates the calm, sending His breath of life into the uniting of an egg and sperm. This is the place life begins. The two united cells begin to divide at an astonishing rate as it journeys from your fallopian tube to your uterus, attaching itself to your uterine wall.

Within the first fourteen days, the placenta is already in place, connected to the fetus by the umbilical cord.

After only twenty-one days, the heart is already beating. Before you even know that you are pregnant, the central nervous system and lungs are developing.

At twenty-eight days, your baby is approximately three-sixteenths of an inch long, and dark circles mark where the eyes will be. Arms and legs begin to form and look like small buds. Tiny ears begin to develop from folds of skin on either side of the head. The brain is developing, and the heart is pumping blood.

By five weeks, the baby is approximately a third of an inch long. The part of the nervous system that handles the equilibrium and spatial relations begin to develop. Facial features are apparent. The mouth has a tongue. Each eye has a retina and lens. The baby can now practice movement because the major muscle system is developed.

All of this happened in the secrecy of your inner most parts. All of this happened before you even realized you were pregnant. The first eight weeks of development are crucial in that the framework for all the internal and external structures are laid. The task is undertaken with great care and skill.

For you created my inmost being; you knit me together in my mother's womb. I praise you because I am fearfully and wonderfully made; your works are wonderful, I know that full well. My frame was not hidden from you when I was made in the secret place. When I was woven together in the depths of the earth, your eyes saw my unformed body. All the days ordained for me were written in your book before one of them came to be. (Psalm 139:13–16)

By eight weeks, the brain and spinal chord are formed. Your baby is now one inch long and legs and arms begin to show the divisions of fingers and toes, though they are short and webbed. Ankles are formed. Wrists are formed. Your child weighs less than one ounce.

Even though you cannot feel its movement, by nine weeks, it is beginning to kick. Your baby may even be getting the hiccups at a rate of up to twenty-eight times per minute. The heart continues to beat more powerfully, gaining strength. Your child can turn its head and open its mouth. Soft fingernails are developed.

By ten weeks, almost every organ is formed, crafted by the Master. Vocal chords are completely developed, and the baby is able to silently cry. The brain is fully formed, and the baby can feel pain. Eyelids now protect the sensitive eyes. The baby has become conversant with its space. Its vestibular (balancing) system in the inner ear is functional. Amazingly, the baby feels every move you make and will attempt to change position accordingly to re-stabilize itself.

Your baby is also able to jump by eleven weeks. The face continues to form, and the eyes begin to move closer together. Hair is growing on your baby's head.

At twelve weeks, your baby is almost three inches long and weighs about one ounce. The external ears have developed. The hands now have fingers, and fingernails are continuing to form. The feet have toes, and toenails are forming. Teeth are developing within the tiny jaw. God knits and weaves all the intricate parts of your baby's physical, emotional, and mental person. With each new life, He creates a new mold; He invents a new pattern, never ending in His creativity. The baby is capable of experiencing many different sensations. It is connected with you physically as well as emotionally. It can receive the things you put into your body as well as sense your emotional state.

Now, at thirteen weeks, your baby can manipulate the movement of its tongue as well as swallow amniotic fluid. Your child's skin is pink and transparent. Within the next week your baby will be able to move its lips and make facial expressions. Just think of your little darling turning up the corners of its mouth, forming a smile. Our Father in Heaven created all the coordinating muscles to do that.

By fifteen weeks, the face is formed and features are well defined. Your baby has taste buds and can distinguish different tastes. Our Creator delights in giving good gifts to us. Why else would he create us with taste buds, allowing us to savor the scrumptious flavors of food? Taste buds give us no other benefit than pleasure. What a thoughtful and loving Creator!

By sixteen weeks, your baby is seven inches long and weighs close to four ounces. Your baby has eyelashes and eyebrows. Your baby can react to visual stimuli from outside of the womb. For instance, if a light were shown on your abdomen, your baby would turn its head away.

At Eighteen weeks, the baby is capable of grasping with its hands. Think of the coordination that is required for such a movement! The internal organs continue to develop. Within the bowel, meconium is accumulating.

By twenty weeks, the baby weighs up to one pound and is almost one foot in length. Typically you begin to feel your baby move inside of you as it exercises and develops it muscles. Your baby begins to hear, and it knows the sound of your voice.

At twenty-two weeks, the baby makes sucking movements. The baby listens to the sounds made by your body.

Imagine what a soothing sound the steady beating of your heart is to the tiny life that grows within you.

By the end of the sixth month, the baby is up to fourteen inches long and weighs as much as two pounds. The brain and lungs continue to grow. Your baby now responds to sound, getting excited by a sudden, loud noise and soothed by your gentle voice. The baby can synchronize its body and eye movements in response to your speech patterns.

By twenty-six weeks, the eyes are completely formed. Now your child no longer has room to turn complete somersaults. Within the next four to six weeks it usually turns head down into the position for birth. The next three months, the baby grows rapidly, gaining lots of weight.

At twenty-seven weeks, your baby can make the movements of breathing, developing the muscles of the chest. Occasionally amniotic fluid might get into the windpipe giving your baby the hiccups. The brain controls breathing and body temperature. Your baby can move its eyes in their sockets. Your child has five functioning senses, even though it is still within your womb, sensitive to sound, light, taste, pain, and smell.

By twenty-nine weeks, the baby responds to sounds outside of the womb by movement and rate of heartbeat. The organs are already developed; the brain has gone through a rapid development, leaving the lungs as the only organ not fully developed. However, if your baby were born at this point, it would be capable of breathing. Movements become more coordinated as the muscles grow. Your baby's bones begin to harden. Your child is approximately fifteen inches long and weighs up to three pounds.

By the eighth month, your baby is eighteen inches long and can weigh up to five pounds. Nails are completely formed and hair continues to grow on your baby's head. God knows your child before it was a glimmer of hope in your eye, and He fashioned your child with just the right temperament for your family. However, now is the time that you typically begin to recognize the individual nature of your baby; your child begins to show signs of personality and purposeful behavior. Though your baby does not move as often, the movements are much stronger.

By thirty-three weeks your baby has two different states of sleep: REM, which is an active dreaming sleep, and deep sleep. Your child's body develops immunities to fight infection.

By thirty-five weeks, the average baby weighs about six and a half pounds. In preparation for the outside world, the baby practices breathing.

At thirty-seven weeks breathing is still unpredictable and random. Now your baby sleeps ninety-five percent of the time and gains approximately one half of a pound per week. The lungs continue to mature.

By the end of your forty weeks, the average baby will weigh seven and a half pounds and measure twenty inches in length. The baby adjusts its position for birth.

This is where the journey begins . . .

Final Thoughts:

Life is a process. Grief is a process. In the midst of this journey, sometimes it feels as though the pain is endless, but I want to give you this encouragement from Philippians: be confident of this that *He who began a good work in you will carry it on to completion until the day of Christ Jesus.* It is a process. There is a beginning, and there is an end. I am so grateful that God exists outside of time; He sees the beginning, the middle, and the end.

Points to Ponder:

As you read through the process of developing life, what emotions rise in you?

In chapter 2, you were asked to *describe how you feel when you think about God, your Creator.* Through these chapters and your journey to this point, have you learned anything new about God?

Describe, again, how you feel when you think about God, your Creator.

Grief is a process; where are you in this process? The beginning, the middle, or the end?

Memorize Philippians 1:6

About the Author

Rebeckah grew up in a small town in northeast Wisconsin. She met her husband while at a missionary training school in Colorado. Adam, originally from Arizona, has worked with youth for more than ten years. The Ripley family currently serves with a missionary organization working in the Middle East and North Africa. Gideon is home schooled.

If you wish to contact Rebeckah, you may email **GideonsMom1998@yahoo.com**. She would welcome the opportunity to hear your story.

Bibliography

Chapter Seven: On Grief

The Grief Continuum: Three Stages of Grief Work, written by Phil Rich, Ed.D., MSW. Original source: *WWW.SelfHelpMagazine.Com*. Used with permission from the publisher and the author. The article is based upon a book by Rich entitled *The Healing Journey Through Grief*. The citation for the book is Rich, P. (1999). New York: John Wiley & Sons.

Chapter Eleven: Acceptance

Original source for *Purified Silver*, unknown.

Permission to use the lyrics from *He's Always Been Faithful*, granted by Sarah Groves.

Emily Perl Kingsley "Welcome to Holland" Jack Canfield, Mark Victor Hansen, Jennifer Read Hawthorne, Marci Shimoff, *Chicken Soup for the Mother's Soul* (Deerfield Beach, Florida: Health Communication, Inc, 1997), pp. 113–114.

Chapter Twelve: Fearfully and Wonderfully Made
Sheila Kitzinger, *Your Baby, Your Way: Making Pregnancy Decisions and Birth Plans.* New York, Pantheon Books, 1987.
George E. Verrilli, M.D., F.A.C.O.G., Anne Marie Mueser, Ed.D., *While Waiting: A Prenatal Guidebook.* New York, St. Martin's Press, 1989.
Fetal Development Calendar from **WWW.MakeWayForBaby.com**.

To order additional copies of

My Child has Special Needs
A JOURNEY FROM GRIEF TO JOY

Have your credit card ready and call:

1-877-421-READ (7323)

or please visit our web site at
www.pleasantword.com

Also available at: www.amazon.com

Printed in the United States
75509LV00002B/47

9 781414 100401